**IMPRIMATUR**
+ Most Reverend Robert J. McManus, S.T.D.
Bishop of Worcester
January 16, 2020

Pflaum Publishing Group
3055 Kettering Blvd., Suite 100
Dayton, OH 45439
800-543-4383
Pflaum.com

ISBN: 978-1-94735-826-3

Printed in China.

A division of Bayard, Inc.

Text by Anne-Sophie du Bouëtiez • Illustrations by Aurélie Abolivier

# The Sacrament of Eucharist

## CELEBRATING THE GIFT OF JESUS

Pflaum.....
SACRAMENTAL PREPARATION

The Bible is the book that recalls the encounter between God and humanity. From its very beginning, it says that God speaks to people and nourishes them.

Knowing they are cared for, God's people respond in faith and trust. But in order to live, people need to be nourished and be loved.

Just as God fed the Chosen People with manna, God's Son, Jesus Christ, feeds his followers, the Christians. During his last meal before dying on the Cross, Jesus wanted to give himself as food for his friends. He asked them to celebrate this same meal again in memory of him.

Since then, every Sunday Catholics gather to pray, sing, and share the bread and wine that is the Body and Blood of Jesus. The bread and wine are Jesus himself who invites us to share his life and to love others as he does.

# God feeds us

"I will take you as my own people, and I will be your God." « *Exodus 6:7* »

# God frees us

In the time of Moses, the Hebrew people were slaves of the Egyptians. But one day God said to Moses, "Moses, I have heard my people, and I want to deliver them. Go ask Pharaoh to let them go."

But Pharaoh refused. So God decided to liberate them. God said, "This night, I will free you. Before leaving, eat a roasted lamb and unleavened bread. Eat in a hurry, with your sandals on your feet."

That night, for the Hebrews, the lamb and the bread were the taste of freedom. To this day, the Jewish people have never forgotten what God did for them that night.

# God restores trust

The Chosen People, who were finally free, walked in the desert. But all of them were hungry, and they began to protest: "We were better off in Egypt. At least there we had something to eat."

Then God said to Moses, "I am going to rain down bread from Heaven for you." And in the morning, something white and thin like frost covered the earth. It was called manna. It tasted good, and every morning it rained down again so that the people were always fed.

The Hebrews continued their journey in the desert with new trust. God was really there for them; they could count on God's faithful help.

## Manna

*Upon seeing this honey-sweet frost, the Hebrews exclaimed, "What is it?" They did not know what the bread of God was.*

13

# The people of God remember

Every year on Passover, Jewish people remember what God did for the Hebrews in the desert. Families gather around to share a meal. Each food is reminiscent of the time the Hebrews left Egypt.

The head of the family takes unleavened bread or matzah, blesses it, and shares it.

As they eat this bread, everyone remembers that the Chosen People were set free by God himself.

**Jewish people**
*Like Christians, Jewish people believe in the same God, but they do not recognize Jesus Christ as the Messiah. Their religion is called Judaism.*

**Passover**
*In Hebrew, Passover means "passage." It is called this because the Angel of Death, who killed the firstborn sons of the Egyptians, passed over the houses of the Jews. They were spared by this "pass over."*

Jesus love

16

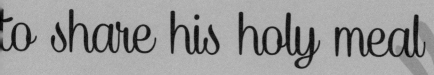

# to share his holy meal

"I am the bread of life; whoever comes to me will never hunger." « *John 6:35* »

# Jesus turns water into wine

One day, Jesus was invited to a wedding in the village of Cana, Galilee. During the meal, someone realized that there was no more wine. Jesus then told the servants to go draw water. When they served it to the guests, the water had become a delicious wine!

This wine was even better than the wine served at the beginning of the meal.

We are invited to Jesus' special meal, which is festive, joyous, and plentiful!

# Jesus shares his meal with the excluded

Jesus entered the city of Jericho, surrounded by a huge crowd. Zacchaeus, a small man, had heard of Jesus and was eager to see who he was, so he climbed a tree. Jesus saw him and said to him: "Zacchaeus, come down. Today I must go and stay at your house!"

Zacchaeus was not well liked because he helped the Romans collect taxes, so the Jewish people, who were enemies of the Romans, accused him of being unjust. Despite this, Jesus wanted to share a meal with him, and Zacchaeus repented of any wrong he had done.

Jesus came for the excluded and for all those who want to change their hearts.

# Jesus feeds a crowd

One day, Jesus was in the middle of a huge crowd.
He spoke to them about God, his Father.

Night came and people were getting hungry.
Jesus could have sent them away, but he wanted
to feed them all. He fed them with five loaves of bread
and two fish, and everyone had enough to eat!

Those who listened to Jesus were hungry for food,
but also for words that would fill their hearts.
The meal that Jesus offered was the beginning
of something extraordinary. Soon, he would offer
his disciples a bread that gives life.

"I have given you a model to follow, so that as I have done for you, you should also do."

« *John 13:15* »

# Jesus washes the feet of his Apostles

Before being condemned to die on the Cross, Jesus shared a last meal with his friends.

In the middle of the meal, he got up, took a cloth, filled a basin of water, and started washing their feet. The Apostles were shocked: that's what servants do! Jesus explained to them, "You call me Master and Lord, and I have washed your feet like a servant. Do the same. Be servants to one another."

By this action, Jesus wanted to make his friends understand that to love is to think of others first and to serve them generously.

**Apostles**
*The Apostles were the twelve special friends that Jesus chose to be with him.*

**Why wash feet?**
*At the time of Jesus, the roads were dusty, and people often walked barefoot. When a person was invited to someone's house, a servant would wash the guest's feet as a sign of respect, but also because it was nice and refreshing!*

# Jesus shares bread and wine

During the last meal which Jesus shared with his Apostles, he took bread, blessed it, and said to them, "Take, eat, this is my body." Then he took a cup, gave thanks, and said, "Take, drink all, for this is my blood that will be shed for you. You will do this in memory of me" (see Matthew 26:26–28).

The Apostles did not yet understand the meaning of Jesus' words.

After his Resurrection, they would understand that Jesus always gave his life—in his words, in the bread and wine, and on the Cross.

# Christians remember

"Do this in memory of me."

« *Luke 22:19* »

Jesus' sacred meal

# Early Christians share the "Lord's Supper"

After Pentecost, Jesus' disciples often met to share the "Lord's Supper." During those meals, one disciple took bread and wine, blessed them, and repeated the words of Jesus.

They felt great joy in this meal and found the strength to go and proclaim the Good News because they felt that Jesus was present in their midst.

We celebrate this meal, too. But what is this supper that nourishes much more than only our bodies?

## Pentecost

*Fifty days after Easter, Jesus' disciples received a special strength. It was the Spirit of God, or the Holy Spirit. The Spirit urged them to go and tell the whole world that Jesus was risen and alive forever.*

## Good News

*By his Resurrection, Jesus conquered death. We, too, are alive forever with him, and our death will not be the end of everything. It will be a passage to a new life with God.*

# We gather today

Two thousand years later, Catholics still come together to celebrate the Lord's Supper. They give thanks and feed on God's Word and the mysterious sacrament of Jesus' Body and Blood.

For Catholics, this gathering is called the Mass or the Eucharistic Liturgy. When we go to Mass, we respond to God's invitation. God wants all his children to meet together in the celebration of the Eucharist.

Sunday Mass has a special place in the lives of Catholics because Jesus was raised on that day. Also, in Latin, *Sunday* means "day of the Lord."

# Thank you!

At Mass, many songs are ways of saying thanks. We sing "Glory to God," "Alleluia," "Hosanna!" This is because the whole Mass is a huge thank you. This is the meaning of the word *Eucharist*.

*Eucharist* comes from a Greek word meaning "to thank." When we celebrate the Eucharist, we thank God, whose love is stronger than evil and death.

# God speaks to us

At Mass, before receiving Communion, we listen
to the Word of God.

Jesus fed the crowds with bread, but also with words
that fill the heart. We are like these crowds: in order
to live, we need to eat, but we also need to hear
words of love.

Jesus' words make us hungry for him. When we listen
to them, we want to get closer to him. After hearing his
words, it is time to share the Lord's meal . . .

# "Take, eat"

During the Eucharist, the priest says, "Jesus took the bread, gave thanks, broke it, and gave it to his disciples saying, 'This is my body, given up for you.' Then he took the cup of wine, again gave thanks, and gave it to his disciples, saying, 'This is the chalice of my blood, the blood of the new and eternal covenant, which will be poured out for you and for many for the forgiveness of sins. Do this in memory of me.'"

The priest says these words and offers the bread and wine in the name of Jesus. This is a way of remembering the last meal that Christ shared with his Apostles, but even more important, the bread and wine become the Body and Blood of Jesus. We believe that today Jesus always gives himself to us in the Eucharist.

**"This is my body"**
*Catholics believe that during Mass the bread and wine become the Body and Blood of Jesus, while still looking like bread and wine. This mystery is called "transubstantiation." We believe that in the Eucharist Jesus is fully present and gives himself to us in love.*

**Host**
*The word host comes from the Latin word meaning "sacrificial victim." This name is given to the bread of Holy Communion.*

41

# Asking forgiveness

Before receiving Communion, we humble ourselves and ask God's forgiveness.

In the Our Father, we pray, "Forgive us our trespasses as we forgive those who trespass against us." We also say, "Lamb of God, have mercy on us."

Sin clutters our lives and separates us from God. But when we turn to God in sorrow, we are embraced and forgiven. Once our hearts are at peace, we are ready to receive Jesus.

**Lamb of God**

*The Jewish people used a lamb as a sacrifice, offered to God in thanksgiving for the blessings received. Jesus is the "Lamb of God" because he sacrificed himself by giving his life for us.*

# The Sign of Peace

We do not always know those who sit near us at Mass. What brings us together is the invitation of Jesus. He loves us as God's children and he wants us to be united. For this to become possible, he gives us his peace.

At Mass, the priest says, "The peace of the Lord be with you always." The people reply, "And with your spirit." Then the priest adds, "Let us offer each other the sign of peace."

In the church, we turn to the people around us, smile, and say, "Peace be with you," perhaps shaking hands with them.

**The peace of Christ**
*In conquering sin and death, Jesus promises to be with us always. Jesus gives us a new and profound peace and then asks us to share it with others.*

# We receive Communion

We come forward to receive Jesus Christ
in Holy Communion.

Communion allows us to be united to one
another and to love like Jesus loved.

The hosts we receive are part of the same bread.
In this way, we are all united as one body.
This is the meaning of the word *communion*.

## Amen

*The priest, deacon, or a extraordinary minister of Holy Communion gives us the host and says, "The Body of Christ." We answer, "Amen." We also may be offered the chalice. The priest, deacon, or a extraordinary minister of Holy Communion says, "The Blood of Christ." We answer, "Amen." In Hebrew this word means, "Yes, it is true. I believe. I believe that Jesus is alive, and that he gives me his life."*

# God sends us forth

After Communion, the priest or deacon tells us, "Go in peace." We leave Mass to share what we have just experienced. We answer, "Thanks be to God." And we go into the world to spread the Good News like the first disciples did.

**All together**
*Mass is an encounter, a sharing. We are not Christians by ourselves. In all his words and all his acts, Jesus wants to teach us to love one another and to serve one another.*

**Mass**
*This word means "sent" in Latin. After receiving the Word of God and the Body and Blood of Christ, we are sent to share with others those things that nourish our lives.*

# I, too, would like to receive Holy Communion

"Whoever remains
in me and I in him
will bear much fruit."

*« John 15:5 »*

# I prepare myself

Maybe you haven't received your First Communion yet, but you would like to participate to feel closer to Jesus.

Through religious formation and with your family, you can prepare for your First Communion. By reading the Gospels, by asking questions, and by paying attention at Mass, little by little, you will discover more about the very special gift that Jesus gives you. Jesus gives us the gift of himself in the Eucharist.

**First Communion**
*Catholics often make their First Communion when they are seven or eight years old. In the Orthodox church, babies receive Communion for the first time on the day of their Baptism. Protestants often wait until they are adults to share in the Lord's Supper for the first time.*

# I receive Holy Communion for the first time

Your First Communion Day is a day of celebration! You have picked out beautiful clothes, and your parents may have prepared a special meal. Your family and your friends are with you.

Today is a special day because today you will get even closer to Jesus.

Jesus is truly present in the host that you will receive. He gives you all his strength and joy and enables you to love as he loves. By receiving Holy Communion, you become united to all Catholics. Together, we form the Body of Jesus Christ.

During your life, each time you receive Holy Communion, you will grow in your love for God and one another.

# Questions

### What is a sacrament?

We cannot see God. But Jesus left us visible signs called sacraments so that we can meet him and know that he is present. A sacrament consists of actions and words that come from God. In the sacraments, God comes to us in person to give us his own divine life that we call grace. The first of the Seven Sacraments is Baptism.

### Why is Holy Communion a sacrament?

For Catholics, Holy Communion is the Body and Blood of Jesus under the appearance of bread and wine. In Communion, Jesus makes himself present to us, as he has promised. This is why Communion is one of the Seven Sacraments.

### Do the bread and wine really turn into Jesus's Body and Blood?

Catholics believe that the bread and wine truly become Jesus' Body and Blood. But they still look, feel, and taste like bread and wine. This is the great mystery of the Eucharist. Jesus is truly present in Holy Communion, also called the Eucharist. He gives us all his life, all his love, and all his presence.

### What does it feel like when we receive Holy Communion?

When you eat the host, it tastes like a very light bread or cracker. But when you receive Holy Communion, you know that Jesus is giving himself to you in a special way. When you receive Jesus, he helps you to be able to love the way he does. After receiving Communion, you can pray for a few minutes to thank him.

### Why don't we use "regular" bread for Communion?

The bread used for Communion is made with flour and water, but without yeast. It called "unleavened bread," and it is used in remembrance of the bread eaten by the Hebrews before leaving Egypt.

### Do we have to receive both the bread and wine at Holy Communion?

No, the Catholic Church says that receiving either the bread or the wine is receiving the entire Body, Blood, Soul, and Divinity of Jesus, but most of the time, we receive either the host alone or both the host and the wine. When you receive Communion, the priest, deacon, or extraordinary minister of Holy Communion will give you the host. You can then go to another minister to drink from the chalice (cup) of wine. You do not have to drink from the chalice if you don't want to.

### Why do we wait until we are seven or older to make our First Holy Communion?

It's not easy to understand what Jesus tells us about his Body and Blood. The Apostles themselves were slow to grasp the meaning of it all. That's why the Catholic Church says it takes time to prepare for Communion.

### How do I know if I am ready to make my First Communion?

You may be afraid you don't understand everything about Communion. But don't worry—you have your whole life to discover how the Eucharist nourishes your heart. If you have studied, and especially if you have the desire, you will know when you are ready.

### How should we receive Communion?

When you are handed the host, you can form a "throne" to receive it by supporting your left hand with your right hand. Then you take the host with your right hand and place it in your mouth. You can also open your mouth to receive the host directly on your tongue. The most important thing about receiving Communion is to be reverent and respectful.